The Delaplaine
2021 Long Weekend Guide

Andrew Delaplaine

NO BUSINESS HAS PAID A SINGLE PENNY OR GIVEN _ANYTHING_ TO BE INCLUDED IN THIS BOOK.

A list of the author's other travel guides, as well as his political thrillers and titles for children, can be found at the end of this book.

Senior Editors - **_Renee & Sophie Delaplaine_**
Senior Writer - **James Cubby**

Gramercy Park Press
New York London Paris

Please submit corrections, additions or comments to
andrewdelaplaine@mac.com

BOSTON
The Delaplaine
Long Weekend Guide

TABLE OF CONTENTS

Chapter 1
WHY BOSTON?

Boston, the largest city in New England and the capital of Massachusetts, is one of the most popular destinations in the U.S. Because of its history, museums, historical sites, and impressive schedule of events, Boston continues to be one of the ten most popular cities to visit in America.

Some of the best museums in the country are located in Boston. Boston's Museum of Fine Arts, one of the largest museums in the U.S., should not be missed and takes at least a day to see the 450,000 works of art. This museum is known for its impressive assortment of French Impressionist paintings and has the largest collection of Monet paintings outside of Paris. Science buffs will not want to miss the Collection of Historical Scientific Instruments, located in Harvard Square, with its collection of over 20,000 objects dating back to 1400. A visit to Boston is not complete without strolling the campus of Harvard University, the site of the **Harvard Art Museums** which are comprised of three museums, the **Fogg Museum,** the **Busch-Reisinger Museum**, and the **Arthur M. Sackler Museum**, as well as four research centers. These museums hold approximately 250,000 objects from all over the world. Tourists continue to flock to the Harvard Museum of Natural History, also on the grounds of Harvard, to see the beautiful "Glass Flowers" collection. The Institute of Contemporary Art, another favorite art stop, is located on Fan Pier on the South Boston Waterfront. **The Isabella Stewart Gardner Museum**, a former villa owned by an eccentric Bostonian, holds an amazing collection of European objects and floral displays. A favorite of scientists and lovers of technology, the MIT Museum houses collections in science, technology, holography, architecture, design, engineering, and history. Another favorite of science lovers is the Museum of Science, located at Science Park Station, with over 700 interactive exhibits. The New England Aquarium, one of the world's largest fish tanks, houses a variety of animals including sharks, sea turtles, stingrays, eels, and barracuda. Those interested in cultural history will want to visit the Peabody Museum of Archeology and Ethnology, one of the oldest museums in the world with a concentration on anthropology. The Semitic Museum features a collection of over 40,000 artifacts from the Near East. The USS Constitution Museum, located in Charlestown Navy Yard just yards from Old Ironsides, features tours and interactive installations. The Warren Anatomical Museum features a collection of unusual and pathological specimens.

Boston is home to some of the world's best art collections with an impressive collection of galleries, many located in the Newbury Street area. **The Panopticon Gallery**, one of the oldest galleries in the U.S. solely focused on photography, specializes in American Photography and emerging contemporary photography. **The Axelle Fine Arts Galerie**, on Newbury Street, features a selection of museum-quality paintings from contemporary European painters.

Visitors return to Boston year after year as it's one of those cities that you can never see everything. Some of the to attractions that visitors should not miss are listed here. The **Skywalk Observatory**, New England's tallest vantage point, gives visitors an amazing 360-degree view of Boston. History buffs love visiting Revolutionary Boston at the Old State House, a house built in 1713, that offers tours and a view of John Hancock's coat. Boston Common, the oldest city park in the U.S., consists of 50 acres and is a popular spot for locals and tourists. The Freedom Trail, a two and a half mile path, passes 16 nationally significant historic sites including the USS Constitution, the Old State House, Boston Common, the Bunker Hill Monument, and Faneuil Hall, the site where the Boston Tea Party was planned. Visit the Boston Harbor Islands National Park Area for a great nature experience where you can enjoy hiking, camping, swimming, picnicking, and fishing. Boston's Harborwalk boasts thirty-nine miles of walkways and boardwalks featuring interpretive displays, art installations, and signs. Sports fans from around the globe travel to Boston just for a chance to see Fenway Park, home of the Boston Red Sox. As corny as it seems, the Boston Duck Tours is one of the most interesting and entertaining ways to see Boston with a ride in the Charles River.

Boson's events draw massive crowds of visitors from around the world. St. Patrick's Day, March 17, is celebrated in full force in Boston since it boasts one of the largest Irish populations outside of Ireland. The Boston Marathon, the third Monday in April, is the

oldest marathon in the world and attracts runners and spectators from around the globe. Boston Pride, scheduled in June, is Boston's second-largest event after the Fourth of July with a weekend filled with events including the parade. Boston celebrates the Fourth of July like no other city in the U.S. boasting the oldest and largest public celebration in the country with the Boston Pops playing for the finale and fireworks. If you're in Boston in August don't miss the Feast of St. Anthony, one of the biggest of several Feasts in the North End, featuring a variety of food vendors, games, music and a parade. In October, The Head of the Charles Regatta, with over 8,000 rowers from around the world competing, is one of the world's largest two-day rowing events.

Boston is a shoppers' paradise with its wealth of shopping districts, malls, boutiques and outlets. One favorite district is Newbury Street, eight blocks of high-end boutiques, salons and galleries. Shoppers should also check out Copley Place, the outdoor kiosks of Faneuil Hall Marketplace, and the shops at Prudential Center in the Back Bay.

Boston boasts some of the best restaurants in the country and you'll be able to find everything from fine dining to street vendors. During the day, check out Faneuil Hall and Quincy Market, two of Boston's oldest marketplaces located in downtown. Both house a variety of mainly touristy shops and eateries. Quincy Market is known for its food stalls from local vendors providing a variety of eats from Italian to Chinese.

Music lovers cannot leave Boston without experiencing the Boston Symphony Orchestra and Boston Pops Orchestra, both performing at Symphony Hall. Right around the corner from the Boston Symphony is the New England Conservatory, the world-famous music school. Boston's theater District is where many Broadway shows preview and a great place to catch a touring show. Boston also offers a variety of local theatrical productions. Counter-Productions Theatre Company offers thought-provoking productions with touring shows in

the Boston area. Mystery Café, America's Original Murder Mystery Dinner Theater, offers great entertainment with mystery, music, food, and audience participation.

Chapter 2
GETTING ABOUT

The "T" references in address lines are to the public transportation system, indicating which stop on the "T."

BOSTON COMMON VISITOR INFORMATION CENTER
148 Tremont St (at Winter; T: Park Street), 617 536-4100
www.bostonusa.com

SHOPS AT PRUDENTIAL VISITOR INFORMATION CENTER

800 Boylston St (Center Court; T: Prudential or Back Bay), 617 536-4100
www.bostonusa.com

The National Park Service also maintains two visitor centers as many of the historic sites in Boston are considered part of the Boston National Historical Park:

DOWNTOWN VISITOR CENTER

15 State St (behind the Old State House between Devonshire and Washington; T: State Street), 617 242-5642
www.nps.gov/bost/index.htm

CHARLESTOWN NAVY YARD VISITOR CENTER

Navy Yard Pier 1 (next to the USS Constitution), 617 242-5601
www.nps.gov/bost/index.htm

Navigating the streets of Boston is difficult if you are not familiar with the area. While other American cities have their streets laid out in a grid (New York, Chicago, Philadelphia, etc.), the modern streets of Boston are a twisty and seemingly incomprehensible maze. Boston in the 1600s was a narrow peninsula surrounded by farmland and distant settlements. Landfill, urban expansion, waves of radical economic change, and new technologies have seen sensible street patterns added on to and collide in less sensible ways. Due to dense development, the older street patterns have largely remained in place without being adapted to their modern surroundings.

In this way, Boston is more similar to old European cities than most typical large American cities that were geometrically planned, expanded into unsettled land, or were mainly settled in the late 20th century. Streets in Boston not only turn of their own volition, but often vanish for no particular reason or change names. If you intend to drive in Boston, a GPS or smartphone with GPS capabilities are essential, because Boston streets and avenues have no rhyme or reason to their layout, and signs are often conspicuously lacking.

BY CAR
Driving is to be avoided if possible, due to traffic congestion, poor parking options, high driving-associated costs, the complexity of navigation, notoriously aggressive drivers, brazen jaywalkers, difficult-to-follow city rules and signage, and the simple fact that Boston, with the exception of neighborhoods on the periphery such as Dorchester and Mattapan, is very compact.

BY PUBLIC TRANSIT

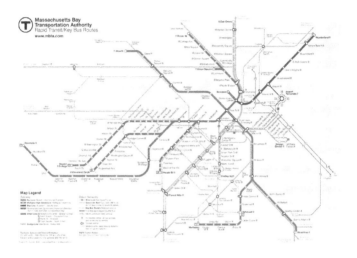

The rapid transit lines of the MBTA system are what you use (Bus, commuter rail, and boat not shown on this map.)

Public transit in Boston is fine for an American city of its size, and is useful in getting around the city, especially considering the issues with driving. A single public transit agency serves the Boston metropolitan area, the **Massachusetts Bay Transportation Authority** ("**MBTA**", or "**the T**" for short). The MBTA is the fourth-largest transit system in the U.S. For complete schedules, maps, and other information, see their web site: www.mbta.com

BY TAXI

Your current alternative to late-night public transit is a taxi. Taxis can be hailed at any significant street corner, such as Kenmore Square or Copley Square. Expect to spend at least $5 and possibly up to $30 in the immediate surroundings (this includes the initial fare, a small tip for the driver, small one-way streets, bad traffic, construction, tolls for bridges, tolls for tunnels, tolls for the Mass Pike, and any wait time). To get further out of Boston, expect to spend much more (for example, from the airport to Wellesley, a Boston suburb, would be around $80, which includes the actual driving and tolls along the way). Fun fact, as of summer 2009, Boston has the most expensive taxis of any major American city.

BY FOOT

Boston's downtown core is compact and easily walkable. Most tourist attractions can be visited on foot, although some neighborhoods require rail and/or bus connections. Take note that while jaywalking is technically illegal, the fine is $1 and tickets haven't been issued for decades. However, if you cross against signals just remember to watch out for stray bikes, cars, and some unusual traffic patterns you won't be used to.

The climate is cold from December to April, and the city is the most windy in America. Snow can also be an obstacle.

If it's late at night, or you feel you cannot deal with the cost of a taxi or the wait involved with the MBTA, then Boston is a relatively small, relatively safe city and walking is an option. Just remember to use the same sense you would in any other city.

BY BICYCLE
Many Boston residents use bicycling as their primary mode of transit all year round, and Boston's small size and relative flatness make biking an appealing way to get around.

Boston lacks many amenities for bicyclists, however, as the roads are covered with potholes and frequently absent of designated bicycle lanes or bicycle racks, so visitors wishing to travel by bicycle should have excellent urban riding skills prior to renting a bicycle.

Cambridge tends to have more bicycle lanes and racks, though many streets still lack them. Riding on the sidewalk is illegal in the city of Cambridge, and frowned upon in Boston, and being well-lit in the evenings is important both for following regulations and for being safe.

A central transit for bikers in Boston is the Southwest Corridor Bike Path, a major park/bike way placed along a route once slated for a major freeway system. This runs parallel to the T's Orange Line and connects Forest Hills to the Back Bay. This is an excellent means of transit if you intend on staying in Jamaica Plain.

In 2011, Boston launched **Hubway** (web site just below), a bike sharing system very similar to those in Washington D.C. and New York City, currently with 61 stations and 600 bicycles. The cost is $5/day, $12/3 day pass, and $85 for a yearly membership.

BOSTON BICYCLE (Cambridge Bicycle), 617-876-6555
www.cambridgebicycle.com/rentals

URBAN ADVENTOURS, 103 Atlantic Ave, 617 670-0637
www.urbanadventours.com

Offers guided bicycle tours for various skill levels. Also provides bike rentals and bike deliveries.

BLUE BIKES
No phone
www.bluebikes.com
2,500 bikes. 260+ stations. 4 municipalities.

Chapter 3
WHERE TO STAY

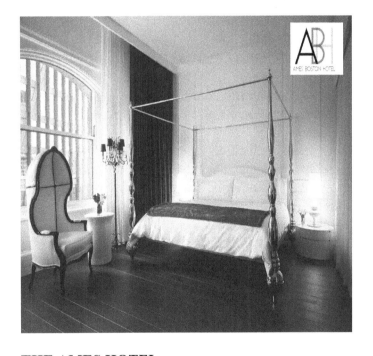

THE AMES HOTEL
1 Court St (between Washington St & State St),
Boston, 617-979-8100
www.ameshotel.com

NEIGHBORHOOD: Downtown
Located in the historic Ames building, this 114-room hotel combines modern style and old world sophistication in its elegant décor. Luxury accommodations include a state-of-the-art fitness center. A non-smoking hotel. Conveniently located near Faneuil Hal and Beacon Hill. Part of the Morgans Hotel Group that owns the Delano on South Beach.

THE CHARLES HOTEL
1 Bennett St., Cambridge, 617-864-1200,
www.charleshotel.com
NEIGHBORHOOD: Harvard Square
Located in the heart of Harvard Square, this spacious hotel offers beautiful contemporary rooms. Amenities include: complimentary Wi-Fi, DVD players, and flat-screen TVs.
Hotel facilities include:
Hotel facilities include: Library, spa, cocktail bar, jazz club, 2 restaurants, sauna, indoor pool, and fitness center.

FAIRMONT COPLEY PLAZA
138 St James Ave, Boston, 617-267-5300
www.fairmont.com/copley-plaza-boston
NEIGHBORHOOD: Harvard Square
A hotel with one of the best locations in town, here in historic Back Bay, this 1912 grande dame offers luxurious accommodations. Concierge floor amenities include: complimentary breakfast, evening hors d'oeuvres, 46-inch flat-screens, high-end coffee machines, and complimentary Wi-Fi access. Hotel

features include: 24-hour fitness center and conference center. Conveniently located blocks from Newbury Street.

FOUR SEASONS HOTEL BOSTON
200 Boylston St (between Charles St & Hadassah Way), Boston, 617-338-4400
www.fourseasons.com/boston
NEIGHBORHOOD: Back Bay
As one of Boston's finest hotels, this luxury Four Seasons Hotel offers 273 guestrooms, including 77 luxury suites, Many of the suites overlook Boston's historic Public Garden and include high speed Internet access. Other amenities include the state-of-the-art fitness center, the 44-foot indoor pool and whirlpool. Guests can dine at the hotel's onsite restaurant, The Bristol Lounge.

HOTEL COMMONWEALTH
500 Commonwealth Ave, Boston, 617-933-5000
NEIGHBORHOOD: Back Bay
www.hotelcommonwealth.com/
Located opposite Kenmore Station, this upscale hotel is opposite Kenmore Station offers elegant accommodations with features like marble bathrooms. Amenities include: flat-screen TVs, DVD players and iPod docks, and complimentary Wi-Fi. Hotel features include: Exercise room, on-site restaurant, oyster bar and cocktail bar. Pet-friendly hotel.

INTERCONTINENTAL BOSTON
510 Atlantic Av (between Fort Hill wharf & Aldine St), Boston, 617-747-1000

www.intercontinentalboston.com
NEIGHBORHOOD: Waterfront, South Boston
The InterContinental Boston Hotel, a new symbol of
elegance and luxury on the Boston Waterfront. The
424 guest rooms & suites of this 5 star hotel are
conveniently located close to the Boston Commons,
Faneuil Hall, Quincy Market, North End, Logan
Airport, Boston Convention Center and other
downtown Boston attractions.

THE LANGHAM, BOSTON
250 Franklin St (at Oliver St), Boston, 617-451-1900
www.boston.langhamhotels.com
NEIGHBORHOOD: Financial District
Originally the building of the Federal Reserve Bank,
this AAA four-diamond Boston hotel is now a
national architectural landmark. The hotel overlooks

the gardens of Post Office Square and is steps from Boston's shops, restaurants and attractions such as Faneuil Hall, Newbury Street, the Freedom Trail, and the financial district. Cafe Fleuri inside is now known as one of Boston's finest restaurants and is known for its Saturday Chocolate Bar Buffet and Sunday Jazz brunch.

LIBERTY HOTEL
215 Charles St, Boston, 617-224-4000
www.libertyhotel.com
NEIGHBORHOOD: Downtown
Set in what used to be the Charles Street Jail, this place housed some of Boston's most notorious criminals for over 120 years. (The building went up in 1859.) Preservationists, architects and historians collaborated on its conversion into this great hotel. Catwalks and a few of the jail cells are still here to be seen. This luxury hotel offers 298 beautiful contemporary rooms and suites – all with floor-to-ceiling windows. Amenities include: flat-screen TVs, and complimentary Wi-Fi. The hotel boasts five restaurants and bars and a 24-hour fitness center.

MANDARIN ORIENTAL BOSTON
776 Boylston Street, Boston, 617-535-8888
www.mandarinoriental.com/boston/
NEIGHBORHOOD: Back Bay
One of Mandarin Oriental's luxury hotels, this Asian inspired luxury hotel offers beautiful rooms, on-site dining, and a 16,000 sq ft spa. Amenities include: complimentary Wi-Fi, flat-screen HDTVs, and

designer toiletries. Conveniently located to area attractions.

NEWBURY GUEST HOUSE
261 Newbury St (between Gloucester St & Fairfield St), Boston, 617-670-6000
www.newburyguesthouse.com
NEIGHBORHOOD: Back Bay
The 32-room is in a brownstone on Newbury Street, and combines quaint touches like brick fireplaces with clean design.

NINE ZERO HOTEL, a KIMPTON HOTEL
90 Tremont St (between Somerset St & Beacon St), Boston, 617-772-5800

www.ninezero.com
NEIGHBORHOOD: Downtown
Located in the heart of the city across from Boston Common, this luxury Kimpton boutique hotel is one of the top hotels in the region. The hotel offers 190 luxury, design-forward guestrooms. Four-star amenities include: hosted evening wine hour, pet-friendly accommodations, wireless Internet, in-room spa services, bikes for exploring the city, and complimentary morning coffee.

OMNI PARKER HOUSE
60 School St (between Beacon St & Tremont St), Boston, 617-227-8600
www.omniparkerhouse.com
NEIGHBORHOOD: Downtown
The oldest hotel in America. Located in downtown Boston on the Freedom Trail, the venerable Omni Parker House Hotel opened its doors in 1855. If you want to surround yourself in history in the heart of Downtown Boston, this is THE place to stay. However, note that many of the hotel's rooms are small and over-crowded with furniture. Bonus: If you eat in the dining room, ask to sit in the booth in which JFK asked Jackie O to marry him.

PARK PLAZA HOTEL & TOWERS
50 Park Plaza (between Hadassah Way & Arlington St), Boston, 617-426-2000
www.bostonparkplaza.com/index.php
NEIGHBORHOOD: Back Bay
A member of the Historic Hotels of America, The Boston Park Plaza has welcomed numerous U.S. presidents and foreign dignitaries. The hotel is located in Boston's Back Bay neighborhood adjacent to the Boston Public Gardens. The hotel features 941 guest rooms and 38 meeting and conference rooms totaling 14,000 square feet of meeting space.

THE NEW RITZ CARLTON
10 Avery St (at Haymarket Place), Boston, 617-574-7100
www.ritzcarlton.com
NEIGHBORHOOD: Chinatown

In the Theater District directly across the Common from the original Ritz-Carlton. Relatively new hotel with a very modern design.

SHERATON BOSTON HOTEL
39 Dalton St, Boston, 617-236-2000
www.sheratonbostonhotel.com/
NEIGHBORHOOD: Back Bay
Located next to the Shops at the Prudential Center, this upscale hotel offers 1,226 newly renovated rooms. Amenities include: Wi-Fi (fee) and flat-screen TVs. Guest staying in club rooms receive access to lounge with free continental breakfast, snacks and afternoon appetizers. Hotel features include: a bistro, a bar, Starbucks coffee shop, indoor pool, fitness room and spa. The parking fees here are among the highest anywhere, so avoid bringing your car if you can.

TAJ BOSTON
15 Arlington St, Boston, 617-536-5700
http://www.tajhotels.com/Luxury/City-Hotels/Taj-Boston-Boston/Overview.html
NEIGHBORHOOD: Back Bay
This is the original Ritz-Carlton, and is located right in the heart of downtown Boston on the Newbury Street side. It's now a Taj Hotel, but still might be considered one of the best in town. occupies the city's most prestigious address at Arlington and Newbury Streets. Renowned for its classic style and award-winning service, this 1927 landmark hotel overlooks the picturesque Public Garden with swan boat rides

and the Boston Common's ice-skating at Frog Pond. Surrounded by art galleries, boutiques and restaurants, the hotel is ideally located near the Theatre District, historic sites, shopping at Copley Place and the Hynes Convention Center. This iconic building underwent a complete restoration in 2002 to celebrate its 75th anniversary. Its prized collection of art and antiques is on display throughout the hotel. There are 273 rooms, including 44 suites that still have wood-burning fireplaces.

W BOSTON
100 Stuart St (between Warrenton St & Tremont St), Boston, 617-261-8700

www.wboston.com
Located in Boston's Theater District, this 235-room hotel offers a beautiful décor, state-of-the-art technology and impressive service. Amenities include: high-speed Internet access, 37" flat screen TVs, pet-friendly accommodations, room service, Fitness Center, on-site dining at Market and Munchie Box, and on-site lounge. Conveniently located near the historical Boston Common. Smoke-free rooms.

Chapter 4
WHERE TO EAT

75 CHESTNUT
75 Chestnut St (between Charles St & Cedar Lane
Way), Boston, 617-227-2175
www.75chestnut.com
CUISINE: American
DRINKS: Full Bar
SERVING: Dinner
PRICE RANGE: $$
NEIGHBORHOOD: Beacon Hill
A cozy antidote to the tourist trap that is the "Cheers"
bar is around the corner. Tucked on a romantic side
street, this dimly lighted restaurant feels like a
modern take on an old brownstone, with tin ceilings
and mahogany pillars.

ALDEN & HARLOW

40 Brattle St, Cambridge, 617-864-2100

www.aldenandharlow.com

CUISINE: American
DRINKS: Full Bar
SERVING: Dinner during the week, Breakfast &
Lunch Sat & Sun
PRICE RANGE: $$$
NEIGHBORHOOD: Harvard Square

Rustic subterranean eatery features Chef Michael
Seelfo's creative menu of American fare. Menu
favorites include: Chicken Fried local rabbit and
Crispy Berkshire Pork Belly with kumquats. Great
spot for brunch.

ASTA

47 Massachusetts Ave, 617-585-9575

www.astaboston.com

CUISINE: American (New)
DRINKS: Wine Bar
SERVING: Dinner; Closed Sun & Mon
PRICE RANGE: $$$$
NEIGHBORHOOD: Back Bay

Upscale New American eatery with fixed-price
tasting-menu. They recently offered a BLT for
dinner, for example. Great, huh? Brick-accented walls
and high ceiling typify this charming eatery that
manages to bridge the gap between a mom-and-pop
joint with fine dining—without missing a beat or even
the slightest hint of pretension. Not an easy task these
days. Choose from 5 or 8 course dinners. Favorites:
Jerk Chicken and Veal with Green Tomatoes.

Selection of meat-free dishes. But you'll want to go for the 8-course dinner. A great experience in a super casual, low stress atmosphere.

B&G OYSTERS
550 Tremont St, Boston, 617-423-0550
www.bandgoysters.com
CUISINE: Seafood, Italian
DRINKS: Beer & Wine Only
SERVING: Lunch, Dinner
PRICE RANGE: $$$
NEIGHBORHOOD: South End
Chef Barbara Lynch offers a modern twist on the classic oyster bar. Menu includes fresh oysters from both coasts, seasonal seafood dishes and New England classics. Menu favorites include: Fried oysters and Atlantic Blue Cod.

BAMBARA
25 Edwin H Land Blvd, Cambridge, 617-868-4444
www.bambara-cambridge.com
CUISINE: American/Juice Bar/Armenian
DRINKS: Full Bar
SERVING: Breakfast, Lunch & Dinner
PRICE RANGE: $$
NEIGHBORHOOD: East Cambridge
Located in the **Hotel Marlowe**, this eatery offers creative cuisine Armenian influence. Favorites: Braised cod with chorizo and Lobster omelet. Great place to grab breakfast or lunch with friends. Crafted cocktails.

BAR LYON
1750 Washington St, 617-904-4020
www.barlyon.com
CUISINE: French
DRINKS: Full Bar
SERVING: Dinner
PRICE RANGE: $$
NEIGHBORHOOD: South End
Casual and much-loved eatery with the atmosphere of an authentic French Bistro. But it's not all show, folks. The food authentically replicates a bistro, the difference being that the quality here is far better than you'll find in your typical French bistro. Favorites like Vichyssoise with crème fraiche; Steak tartare; Chicken liver parfait with red onion marmalade (that's what I mean about being "better"); Duck confit with Lyonnaise potatoes, garlic butter & Vidalia onion (Vidalia onion?—see, that's "better"); a traditional Omelette cooked in the French style, soft & fluffy, not the way Americans ruin an omelette, ending up with a slab of hard-cooked eggs; Mussels, Scallops and a whole lot more. Some people say this is the best French onion soup in town, but I heartily disagree. It IS the best French onion soup in town, period. Also, great burgers. Nice wine selection.

BAR MEZZANA
360 Harrison Ave, Boston, 617-530-1770
www.barmezzana.com
CUISINE: Italian/Seafood
DRINKS: Full Bar
SERVING: Dinner
PRICE RANGE: $$$

NEIGHBORHOOD: South End
Neighborhood eatery (very few tourists) offering a
creative Italian/Seafood menu. Favorites: Grilled
octopus and Beef tartare. Great cocktails and
impressive beer list.

THE BASEBALL TAVERN
1270 Boylston St, Boston, 617-867-6526
www.baseballtavern.com
CUISINE: Sports Bar
DRINKS: Full Bar
SERVING: Lunch & Dinner
PRICE RANGE: $
NEIGHBORHOOD: Fenway
A great spot to stop before a Sox game as it's located
right across from Fenway Park. This place has two
floors, a basement and a rooftop deck. A great place
to hang out if you don't have tickets.

BASTILLE KITCHEN CAFÉ
49 Melcher St, Boston, 617-556-8000
www.bastillekitchen.net
CUISINE: French
DRINKS: Full Bar
SERVING: Dinner
PRICE RANGE: $$$
NEIGHBORHOOD: South Boston/Waterfront
Former factory converted into a French bistro.
Favorites: Bacon wrapped rabbit and French onion
soup. Nice wine pairings. Reservations
recommended.

BISTRO DU MIDI

272 Boylston St (between Hadassah Way &
Arlington St), Boston, 617-426-7878
www.bistrodumidi.com
CUISINE: French
DRINKS: Full Bar
SERVING: Lunch & Dinner
PRICE RANGE: $$$
NEIGHBORHOOD: Back Bay

The Boston-New York inferiority complex is nothing
new, especially when it comes to restaurants. But
Boston has raised its culinary game recently. Opened
last November, this bistro is run by Robert Sisca,
formerly the executive sous chef at Le Bernardin,
who has created a Provençal menu with a focus on
local fish. Favorites include the sweet and spicy pan-
roasted cod with chorizo, chickpeas, pimentos and
golden raisins ($28). Ask to be seated upstairs, where
businessmen and dolled-up couples sit in buttery
yellow leather chairs and gaze at unbeatable views of
the Public Garden outside.

BLUE DRAGON

324 A St, Boston, 617-338-8585
www.bluedragonbos.com
CUISINE: Asian Fusion

DRINKS: Full Bar
SERVING: Lunch & Dinner; closed Sun
PRICE RANGE: $$
NEIGHBORHOOD: Waterfront, South Boston
Small upscale Asian eatery that offers Chef Ming
Tsai's menu of snacks, noodles, banh mi and dim
sum. Menu picks include: Pork & Scallion wontons
and Dan Dan noodles.

BOSTON CHOPS

1375 Washington St, Boston, 617-227-5011

www.bostonchops.com

CUISINE: Steakhouse

DRINKS: Full Bar
SERVING: Dinner nightly, Lunch on Sat
PRICE RANGE: $$$
NEIGHBORHOOD: South End
Popular upscale steakhouse with an impressive menu
and a wine room boasting some 2,000 bottles. Steaks
are cooked sous vide and finished beautifully in a cast
iron skillet. (I love that sizzle.) Yum. Raw bar. Great
selection for weekend brunch.

BRASSICA KITCHEN + CAFÉ

3710 Washington St, 617-477-4519
www.brassicakitchen.com
CUISINE: American (New)
DRINKS: Full Bar
SERVING: Breakfast (Mon-Fri 6-4), Lunch/brunch
each afternoon; Dinner from 5:30
PRICE RANGE: $$
NEIGHBORHOOD: Jamaica Plain
Hip cafe with brick walls decorated with lots of
pictures focusing on breakfast and brunch but also
serving lunch. Euro-style fare with gourmet coffees
and pastries. Favorites: Fried chicken sandwich
(better than it sounds); and Chicken Parm.

BRONWYN

255 Washington St, Somerville, 617-776-9900
www.bronwynrestaurant.com
CUISINE: German
DRINKS: Full Bar
SERVING: Dinner, Late Night
PRICE RANGE: $$$
With the atmosphere of an outdoor Biergarten, Chef
Tim Wiechmann offers a unique German dining
experience. Menu favorites include: Beer-braised
pork shanks and Hand-cased sausages. Here you'll
find an extensive list of German, Austrian, Czech and
Polish beers.

CAFÉ DU PAYS

233 Cardinal Medeiros Ave, 617-314-7297
www.cafedupays.com
CUISINE: French / French-Canadian

DRINKS: Full Bar
SERVING: Dinner; Closed Mondays
PRICE RANGE: $$
NEIGHBORHOOD: Cambridge
Comfortable café with white chairs pushed up against the wooden tables giving the place an almost home-like ambience offering French-Canadian cuisine. Favorites: Poutine; Bluefish with fennel and nardello peppers; and Duck Breast, juicy and tender, with plum sauce; Pork loin, moist & bursting with flavor, with corn and squash. Domestic-feeling dining option for French-Canadian cuisine & spirits in antique-filled room. (and all those white chairs, which are not antiques!) Almond cake with strawberries is a great dessert. Nice wine selection.

CAFE SUSHI
1105 Massachusetts Ave, 617-492-0434
www.cafesushicambridge.com
CUISINE: Sushi Bar, Japanese
DRINKS: Wine & Saki
SERVING: Lunch, & Dinner, Dinner only on Sundays
PRICE RANGE: $$
NEIGHBORHOOD: Cambridge / Harvard Square
For several decades, they've been serving authentic Japanese cuisine and fresh sushi—it's reasonably priced & offers daily specials. Signature Sashimi plates, Bento Boxes and Japanese Hot-Pot dishes. Favorites: Maki rolls and Hamachi Kama (broiled fish collar with daikon and lemon). Chef offers omakase selection as well. Traditional sushi counter with tables out in the room. Dimly lit at night.

CASK 'N FLAGON

62 Brookline Ave, Boston, 617-536-4840

www.casknflagon.com

CUISINE: American/Sports Bar
DRINKS: Full Bar
SERVING: Lunch & Dinner
PRICE RANGE: $$
NEIGHBORHOOD: Fenway

Popular sports bar with 50 or 60 TV screens. Don't come in here unless you're a Sox fan! Tasty bar fare such as fish tacos and ribs – a locals' favorite. But they also have a substantial dinner menu. Great selection of beers – local and national – on draft and in the bottle.

CELESTE

21 Bow St, 617-616-5319

www.celesteunionsquare.com

CUISINE: Peruvian, Latin American, Seafood
DRINKS: Full Bar
SERVING: Dinner – Mon – Sat, Lunch on Sat, Closed on Sundays
PRICE RANGE: $$
NEIGHBORHOOD: Somerville

Modern intimate eatery serving some of the best ceviche and Peruvian cuisine in a simple storefront with some chairs at a counter and a few simple tables. (Full bar helps.) I've always thought the Peruvians treated seafood better and more creatively than any other Latin American culture. This place doesn't nothing to alter my opinion but only reinforces it. Favorites: Tuna tartare and Squid ink linguini with seared scallops. Creative cocktails. The owners here ran a little restaurant from their home before opening in this spot.

CHARLIE'S KITCHEN
10 Eliot St, Cambridge, 617-492-9646
www.charlieskitchen.com
CUISINE: American
DRINKS: Full Bar
SERVING: Dinner & Late Night
PRICE RANGE: $
NEIGHBORHOOD: Harvard Square
It turns out Mr. Clinton wasn't the only recent president to search out a good burger and cheap beer during his study breaks. In Cambridge, Mass., George W. Bush spent time earning his M.B.A. and relaxing

at Charlie's Kitchen, a Harvard staple that also claims visits from President Obama during his time at the school. "Everybody goes to Charlie's," said Helen Metros, who at 83 has been waiting tables there for 54 years. She recalled slinging burger specials to Mr. Bush and countless other political names. "Some students can be know-it-alls," she said, but Mr. Bush was "always a gentleman." On the main floor,

Charlie's has tables with distinctive red-and-black tops and the aura of a classic dive. Head upstairs for a more barlike feeling and a jukebox featuring local bands like Hallelujah the Hills. Jaap Overgaag, the manager, said that people try to persuade him to move to a digital jukebox, but he's resisted since the smaller local acts would be excluded. Try the double cheeseburger.

CHICKADEE
21 Drydock Ave, 617-531-5591
www.chickadeerestaurant.com
CUISINE: American (New), Mediterranean
DRINKS: Full Bar
SERVING: Lunch, & Dinner; Brunch on Sat & Sun.
PRICE RANGE: $$$
NEIGHBORHOOD: Seaport
Located in the Innovation and Design Building, this eatery offers a creative menu with a heavy New England influence. Favorites: Rohan Duck and Grilled Maine Swordfish. Save room for their carrot cake, which I can only describe as a masterpiece of moistness & flavor.

COPPA ENOTECA
253 Shawmut Ave, Boston, 617-391-0902
www.coppaboston.com
CUISINE: Italian/Tapas
DRINKS: Full Bar
SERVING: Lunch, Dinner
PRICE RANGE: $$$
NEIGHBORHOOD: South End

Located on a quiet side street, this eatery features a menu of small Italian plates made with locally sourced ingredients. Menu favorites include: House made pastas and wood fired pizza. The chef emphasizes local ingredients, even to the point that when you eat his lamb with pasta, ragu and Pecorino, you can be sure the mint added to it came from the same pasture where the lamb was raised. There's also a late-night menu served after 11 with items like salt cod crostini and charcuterie platters made in-house. Creative cocktail menu.

CRAIGIE ON MAIN

853 Main St, Cambridge, 617-497-5511
www.craigieonmain.com/
CUISINE: French/American (New)
DRINKS: Full Bar
SERVING: Dinner nightly
PRICE RANGE: $$$$
NEIGHBORHOOD: Central Square Station
Chef Tony Maws – labeled one of America's Best New Chefs by Food & Wine magazine – offers his French inspired seasonal menu. This guy does a lot of the heavy lifting himself, breaking down the carcasses of several whole pigs and a couple of goats as well as 20 or 25 squabs. He's one of those "snout to tail" chefs, using everything the poor animal has to offer. The bones end up in stockpots. The offal ends up in sausages. My favorite dish here is the 3-way lamb (you get it with the neck slow roasted, the tongue prepared confit style and the loin section crusted with spices). The lamb sausage with poached figs is a

standout. Other favorites include Squid ink pasta and Stuffed chicken.

CUCHI CUCHI
795 Main St, Cambridge, 617-864-2929
www.cuchicuchi.cc
CUISINE: Tapas/Small plates
DRINKS: Full Bar
SERVING: Dinner nightly
PRICE RANGE: $$$
NEIGHBORHOOD: Kendall Square
Known for its menu of global small plates and fruity cocktails, this eatery offers a great romantic dining experience. Dishes are meant to be shared. When I say "global" small plates, I mean it. They have dishes that represent cuisines from around the world. Quite an eclectic mix. Great bar menu of signature cocktails.

DAKZEN
195 Elm St, 617-718-1759
www.dakzen.com
CUISINE: Thai
DRINKS: No Booze
SERVING: Lunch, & Dinner (Breakfast on weekends)
PRICE RANGE: $
NEIGHBORHOOD: Somerville / Davis Square
Low-key unprepossessing storefront eatery serving authentic That street food. Don't let the exceedingly simple exterior put you off. Food's the best. Busy counter style service as well as a few tables. If you like hot seasonings on your food, don't miss this

place! Known for their delicious noodles with four different types of broth. Favorites: Khao Moo Dang (Crispy pork belly) and Thai sweet sausage, boiled egg, and cucumber. Note: tipping is optional, but you're expected to get your own utensils and clean your table when finished. (A small thing to ask considering what you're getting in return.)

DELUX CAFÉ
100 Chandler St (between Clarendon St & Columbus Av), Boston, 617-338-5258
No Website
CUISINE: American
DRINKS: Full Bar
SERVING: Dinner
PRICE RANGE: $$
NEIGHBORHOOD: South End

For a younger and cooler scene, check out the Delux Café, a reigning temple of kitsch with walls decorated with records, comic books and a bust of Elvis. To get some New England hipster cred, order a tallboy Narragansett Beer, the region's answer to Pabst Blue Ribbon.

EASTERN STANDARD
528 Commonwealth Ave., Boston, 617-532-9100,
 www.easternstandardboston.com
CUISINE: American (New)
DRINKS: Full Bar
SERVING: Breakfast, Lunch & Dinner
PRICE RANGE: $$
NEIGHBORHOOD: Kenmore Station
Located in Kenmore Square's Commonwealth Hotel, this popular brasserie attracts a bustling late night scene. Revolving selection of late-night specials like Fish tacos, Lamb Carpaccio, and Roasted bone marrow.

FLOUR BAKERY & CAFÉ
12 Farnsworth St, Boston, 617-338-4333
www.flourbakery.com
CUISINE: Bakery, Coffee & Tea
DRINKS: No Booze
SERVING: Breakfast, Lunch
PRICE RANGE: $$
NEIGHBORHOOD: South Boston
This place is much more than a bakery. A long line appears every day to order their exquisite sandwiches: smoked turkey, hummus, curried tuna and roasted

lamb, plus all the usual deli sandwiches, served on crusty baguettes fresh from the oven. Their pastries can't be beat, like the raisin-filled brioche dripping with icing and lemon curd cakes filled with raspberry preserves. The café also serves freshly made salads.

THE GALLOWS
1395 Washington St, Boston, 617-425-0200
www.thegallowsboston.com
CUISINE: French
DRINKS: Full Bar
SERVING: Dinner – Mon –Wed; Lunch & Dinner – Thur - Sun
PRICE RANGE: $$
NEIGHBORHOOD: South End
Trendy gastropub offering flavorful comfort food. They have very good charcuterie boards, Poutine (crispy fries, cheese curd and gravy), or steak frites. Other favorites: Lobster Po'boy and Southern Comfort burger topped with pork, cheese and slaw. Nice cocktail selection. Great place for late-night snacks.

GRILL 23 & BAR
161 Berkeley St, Boston, 617-542-2255
www.grill23.com
CUISINE: Steakhouse
DRINKS: Full Bar
SERVING: Dinner nightly
PRICE RANGE: $$$$
NEIGHBORHOOD: Back Bay
Classy historic steakhouse offers Chef Jay Murray's menu of top-notch steaks and surf 'n' turf classics.

Try the delectable dry aged rib eye with a side of mashed potatoes and you'll be hooked.

GIULIA
1682 Massachusetts Ave, 617-441-2800
www.giuliarestaurant.com
CUISINE: Italian
DRINKS: Full Bar
SERVING: Dinner, Closed Sunday
PRICE RANGE: $$$
NEIGHBORHOOD: Cambridge
Cozy brick-walled eatery offering a menu of Italian classics off Harvard Square. Some of the best pasta in town from a celebrated chef working with a friendly staff. (This is one of those places you like to come in the wintertime because you feel so welcome when you come in out of the cold.) Favorites: Chicken Liver Crostini; Lamb Sausage; Striped Bass; and Pappardelle with Wild Boar (this is always on the menu, whatever else changes, and a lot does). Get the Pistachio Gelato for dessert or share the Warm Almond Torta with someone. Reservations necessary.

THE HAVEN
2 Perkins St, 617-524-2836
www.thehavenjp.com
CUISINE: Gastropubs, Scottish, Fish & Chips
DRINKS: Wine Bar
SERVING: Lunch, & Dinner
PRICE RANGE: $$
NEIGHBORHOOD: Jamaica Plain/Hyde Square
Scottish tavern (with dark-stained tongue-in-groove wainscoting halfway up the wall) featuring a menu of

traditional eats like Fish & Chips. Favorites: Scotch eggs and Chef's Tasting (a four-course meal of whatever the chef feels like making). Eclectic beer and ale list. Occasional live music. Real neighbor feel because, well, it's a neighborhood kind of place.

ISLAND CREEK OYSTER BAR
500 Commonwealth Ave, Boston, 617-532-5300
www.islandcreekoysterbar.com
CUISINE: Seafood
DRINKS: Full Bar
SERVING: Dinner
PRICE RANGE: $$$
NEIGHBORHOOD: Kenmore Square/Fenway
Oyster fans love this place, and for good reason. They get their oysters from Duxbury's Island Creek Oysters, which is the outfit that also supplies top-end eateries like Per Se in New York. The oysters here are fat and juicy and have a super brininess to them,

which I like. I usually get a dozen on the half shell and then get them fried and stuffed into a buttery brioche that they serve as sliders. Other good menu options: Mrs. Bennett's seafood casserole and Pan Fried Jonah crab cake. Book ahead.

JULIET
257 Washington St, 617-718-0958
www.julietsomerville.com
CUISINE: French Cafe
DRINKS: Full Bar
SERVING: Breakfast, Lunch, & Dinner, Closed Mon & Tues
PRICE RANGE: $$
NEIGHBORHOOD: Somerville
Intimate no frills but still high energy Euro-style café with white-tiled walls, high ceilings, offering a pre-fixe as well as a la carte menus. Popular brunch location, with some tables facing the street through high glass windows. Breakfast served all day (try the breakfast taco). Favorites: Wild Chatham mussels; Corn & lobster chowder; Gazpacho (some of the best I've ever had, I think because the olive oil is so good); and Tacos Santa Cruz. Try to avoid the counter where they display the desserts. You'll end up walking out with a whole cake.

KAVA NEO-TAVERNA
315 Shawmut Ave, (617) 356-1100
www.kavaneotaverna.com
CUISINE: Greek
DRINKS: Wine Bar

SERVING: Dinner, Lunch & Dinner on Sat and Sun.
NO RESERRVATIONS
PRICE RANGE: $$$
NEIGHBORHOOD: South End
A crowded little place with counter service and a few
tightly packed tables in an "intimate" neighborhood
eatery offering authentic Greek small plates that has
had people lining up ever since they opened. Quality
Greek food is rare in these parts, so this place is
BUSY, in fact, VERY busy. Go at an off time since
they won't book a table for you. Favorites: Fava and
Octopus; Keftedes (mouthwatering lamb meatballs);
Gavros (white anchovies in olive oil); Sardeles
(grilled anchovies with lemon & olive oil; a Mixed
Grill with lamb chops, chicken skewer, pork skewer
& Greek sausage. Nice selection of wine and spirits.

LA VOILE
261 Newbury St, Boston, 617-587-4200
www.lavoilerestaurants.com/
CUISINE: French
DRINKS: Full Bar
SERVING: Lunch & Dinner
PRICE RANGE: $$$
NEIGHBORHOOD: Back Bay
Intimate upscale eatery serving French fare. Regular
menu and an inexpensive price-fix menu. Favorites:
veal blanquette, Duck and Lamb chops. Great wine
selection. Try the crème Brule – it's topped with fresh
strawberries.

LINCOLN TAVERN & RESTAURANT
425 W Broadway, 617-765-8636

www.lincolnsouthboston.com
CUISINE: American (New)
DRINKS: Full Bar
SERVING: Lunch, & Dinner – Mon – Fri, Brunch on
Sat & Sun
PRICE RANGE: $$
NEIGHBORHOOD: South Boston
Classic, American tavern offering a menu of comfort
dishes. The kind of place Ben Affleck and Matt
Damon would have come to back when they were
"Southies" and before they went Hollywood. Nice
selection of spirits and crafted cocktails. Favorites:
Breakfast pizza and Steak burrito. Popular weekend
brunch destination. In fact, popular all the time.
Typical diner food menu (but good quality) and they
really crank it out. Busy and fun.

LUCKY'S LOUNGE
355 Congress St, Boston, 617-357-5825
https://luckyslounge.com/
CUISINE: American (Traditional)
DRINKS: Full Bar
SERVING: Lunch & Dinner
PRICE RANGE: $$
NEIGHBORHOOD: South Boston/Waterfront
Sinatra-themed lounge with a menu of American
comfort food. (Note: there's not a sign out front).
Favorites: Steakhouse burger and Lucky Cuban 12. A
favorite of locals and hipsters. Classic cocktails.
Popular choice for brunch.

MEI MEI STREET KITCHEN
506 Park Dr, Boston, 857-250-4959
www.MeiMeiBoston.com
CUISINE: Asian Fusion
DRINKS: Beer & Wine Only
SERVING: Lunch & Dinner nightly; Lunch only on Monday
PRICE RANGE: $$$
NEIGHBORHOOD: b/t Buswell St & Beacon St
This food truck and restaurant offers a menu of creative Asian-American fusion fare. Popular dishes include: Fat-braised beef dumplings and Scallion pancake sandwiches.

MENTON
354 Congress St, Boston, 617-737-0099
www.mentonboston.com
CUISINE: French, Italian
DRINKS: Full Bar
SERVING: Dinner
PRICE RANGE: $$$$
NEIGHBORHOOD: South Boston
This popular eatery blends French discipline with Italian passion to create a wonderfully executed menu

for an evening of fine dining. Menton offers two menu options: a four-course prix fixe menu or a seven-course chef's table menu with optional wine pairings. Menus change often. Menu favorites include: Salmon, Monkfish, Venison and Game Hen. Guests are treated to two courses of complimentary desserts along with the prix fixe menus.

MIDA
782 Tremont St, 617-936-3490
www.midaboston.com
CUISINE: Italian, Noodles
DRINKS: Full Bar
SERVING: Dinner, Sunday Brunch
PRICE RANGE: $$$
NEIGHBORHOOD: South End
Neighborhood eatery offering contemporary Italian fare in as clean, sleek interior with high ceilings and

dim lighting at night that gives off a cozier ambience than at lunch, when you can look out the windows at the red-brick row houses across the street. There's seating at the bar. Pastas like Paccheri Bolognese; Lobster scampi over linguini; Spaghetti al granchio. Perfect menu for sharing. A few tables outside, weather permitting. Monday is all-you-can-eat pasta, which is all homemade here.

NO 9 PARK
9 Park St, Boston, 617-742-9991
www.no9park.com
CUISINE: French, Italian
DRINKS: Full Bar
SERVING: Dinner
PRICE RANGE: $$$$
NEIGHBORHOOD: Downtown
Set in an elegant Beacon Hill townhouse with the tables all covered with clean white tablecloths, Chef Barbara Lynch offers a refined menu of French and Italian inspired dishes. This place is known for, and I particularly love, its excellent cheese cart. Try to score a corner table that overlooks Boston Common. If you're on a budget, steer clear of that corner table and opt instead for a seat at the bar where there's a shorter menu that's not nearly as costly as the dining room's. Superior craft cocktails, too. (I like the old-fashioned here.) Menu favorites include: Lamb Saddle and the Prune Stuffed Gnocchi with Foie Gras. Wine list features old world wines.

NEPTUNE OYSTER
63 Salem St (between Hull St & Stillman St), Boston,
617-742-3474
www.neptuneoyster.com
CUISINE: Seafood
DRINKS: Beer & Wine Only
SERVING: Lunch & Dinner
PRICE RANGE: $$$
NEIGHBORHOOD: North End
It's a cliché for a reason: you can't visit Boston, smell
a salt breeze and not want to eat seafood. Steer clear
of the waterfront traps and head to a tiny spot where
Sam Adams-swilling frat boys rub shoulders with
fabulous Champagne sippers at the marble bar. The
attraction? Why, the lobster roll, a mountain of warm,
butter-slicked lobster piled into a soft brioche bun,
with a side of crispy, skin-on fries. For lighter fare,
try yellowtail sashimi on a bed of kimchi and an array
of clams and oysters plucked from nearby waters.

OLEANA

134 Hampshire St., Cambridge, 617-661-0505

www.oleanarestaurant.com

CUISINE: Mediterranean
DRINKS: Beer & Wine Only
SERVING: Lunch & Dinner; closed Sun & Mon
PRICE RANGE: $$$
NEIGHBORHOOD: Inman Square

A popular spot serving inventive Eastern Mediterranean fare. Known for their great falafels but a meal isn't complete without their famous Baked Alaska.

O YA

9 East St., Boston, 617-654-9900

https://o-ya.restaurant/

CUISINE: Japanese
DRINKS: Full Bar
SERVING: Dinner; closed Sun & Mon
PRICE RANGE: $$$$
NEIGHBORHOOD: South Boston

This popular downtown eatery offers an inventive menu of Japanese small plates and delicious sushi. If you're hungry try the 18-odd course omakase menu. Popular dishes include Salmon with wasabi tobiko and Pan-seared foie gras nigiri. Reservations recommended.

PABU

3 Franklin St, Boston, 857-327-7228

www.pabuizakaya.com

www.michaelmini.net
CUISINE: Japanese
DRINKS: Full Bar
SERVING: Lunch & Dinner; Dinner only on Sat;
closed Sun
PRICE RANGE: $$$
NEIGHBORHOOD: Downtown
Located in the heart of Boston's Downtown Crossing
neighborhood, this popular eater offers Michael
Mina's modern twist on traditional Izakaya-style
dining he grew famous for in San Francisco. The fish
served here comes not only from the Atlantic waters
offshore, but from Japan's famous Tsukiji market.
Favorites: Miso-cured black cod, pork belly with
softshell crab, whole Maine lobster mixed with clam
& enoki in a hot pot and Seared Hudson Valley foie
gras. Great upscale dining experience.

PAGU
310 Massachusetts Ave, 617-945-9290
www.gopagu.com
CUISINE: Japanese, Spanish
DRINKS: Wine & Sherry
SERVING: Lunch, & Dinner, Sunday Brunch
PRICE RANGE: $$$
NEIGHBORHOOD: Cambridge
Comfortable eatery offering Japanese & Spanish
small plates and an ever-changing seasonal menu. A
huge counter wraps around the open kitchen on three
sides, so a lot of people can sit and observe. Bare
wooden tables are placed in the rest of the room and
in another room off to the side. There's a separate bar
for drinks (thank you, God). Favorites: Squid ink

Bao; Pork Belly Bao with pickled cucumber; an excellent Spanish omelet; and Cedar Campfire Black Cod.

PAMMY'S

928 Massachusetts Ave, 617-945-1761
www.pammyscambridge.com
CUISINE: Italian, American (New)
DRINKS: Full Bar
SERVING: Dinner; Closed Sunday
PRICE RANGE: $$$
NEIGHBORHOOD: Cambridge / Central Square
Chic American Trattoria offering Italian classics in a room with white-tiled accents and a dark beamed roof creating a cozy, friendly ambience. The ferns, plants, flowers and other growing things scattered throughout really give the place a special feeling. Nice bar scene before you sit down for dinner. All pastas are housemade from flour that's actually milled right here on site. (When did you last see that?) Favorites: the Bolognese sauce here has a touch of gochujang (a Korean red chili paste that imparts a bit of sweetness); Bucatini with grilled shrimp & pistachio; Cavatelli with anchovies. A very good wine selection is available. Altogether a lovely place.

THE PARAMOUNT

667 E Broadway, Boston, 617-269-9999
www.paramountboston.com
CUISINE: American (New)
DRINKS: Beer & Wine
SERVING: Breakfast, Dinner, Lunch
PRICE RANGE: $$

NEIGHBORHOOD: South Boston
Well-known eatery offers comfort food cafeteria-style for breakfast & lunch but full service at night. Favorites: Caramel and banana French toast and Marinated grilled pork loin.

PARKER'S RESTAURANT
OMNI PARKER HOUSE HOTEL
60 School St (between Beacon St & Tremont St), Boston, 617-227-8600
www.omnihotels.com/FindAHotel/BostonParkerHouse se.aspx
CUISINE: American
DRINKS: Full Bar
SERVING: Lunch & Dinner
PRICE RANGE: $$$

In Boston, at Parker's Restaurant, we found another table claimed by its owner to be where John F. Kennedy proposed to Jacqueline Bouvier — 441 miles from the table at Martin's. Sitting at corner table No. 40, we wondered how it could be that he proposed in both places, while still others suggest he proposed by telegram. Unlike Martin's table, the purported proposal spot at Parker's has a low profile: unmarked, it looks out inconspicuously over an arabesque dining room.

Engagement confusion aside, Boston's Parker House Hotel is still an appropriate stop on a presidential pub-crawl. Here, at what is said to be the oldest continuously operating full-service hotel in the United States, Kennedy had a bachelor party and also announced his bid for Congress — although not on the same day. The Vietnamese Communist leader Ho Chi Minh once baked bread for a living at the Parker House. Today, visitors can enjoy two great bars and, of course, the signature Parker House rolls.

PURITAN & COMPANY

1166 Cambridge St, Cambridge, 617-615-6195
www.puritancambridge.com
CUISINE: American (New)
DRINKS: Full Bar
SERVING: Dinner nightly, Lunch Sat & Sun
PRICE RANGE: $$$
NEIGHBORHOOD: Inman Square
They offer a very creative menu of New American fare that packs this little place. Lovely items such as swordfish pastrami, scallop crudo (so delicate),

glazed lamb belly with eggplant. Great place for brunch. Incredible pastries. (Get the mint oreo for dessert.)

ROSEBUD AMERICAN KITCHEN & BAR
381 Summer St, Somerville, 617-629-9500
www.rosebudkitchen.com
CUISINE: Southern/American (Traditional)
DRINKS: Full Bar
SERVING: Dinner, Lunch Fri-Sun
PRICE RANGE: $$
NEIGHBORHOOD: Davis Square
Former iconic diner (dating back to 1941) transformed into a family-friendly eatery offering a menu of traditional Southern/American comfort food. Favorites: Loaded Mac & Cheese, St. Louis style ribs, fried chicken, Texas brisket and Grilled Swordfish are hard to beat. Save room for one of their specialty desserts.

ROW 34
383 Congress St, Boston, 617-553-5900
www.row34.com

CUISINE: American (New), Seafood
DRINKS: Beer & Wine Only
SERVING: Lunch, Dinner
PRICE RANGE: $$$
NEIGHBORHOOD: Waterfront
A workingman's bar, this place is known for its great oysters and unique beers. Opened by the same people behind the famous **Island Creek** over in the Kenmore square area. Great raw bar. Menu favorites include: Homemade bucatini with clams and Shrimp sliders. Very busy so reservations are definitely recommended.

SALTIE GIRL
281 Dartmouth St, 617-267-0691
www.saltiegirl.com
CUISINE: Seafood, Cocktail Bar
DRINKS: Full Bar
SERVING: Lunch, & Dinner
PRICE RANGE: $$$
NEIGHBORHOOD: Back Bay
Seafood eatery offering a varied menu including fresh seafood, raw bar, lobster rolls, crudo, shellfish platters, New York style smoked fish, French snails with black butter; Fried whole belly Ipswich clams; Tinned fish, and Caviar. Raw bar. Favorite lunch spot after shopping Newbury Street. Grab a seat at the always busy counter or one of the tables squeezed in against the walls. Either way, lots of fun and really great food.

SARMA
249 Pearl St, Somerville, 617-764-4464

www.sarmarestaurant.com
CUISINE: Middle Eastern/Moroccan/Turkish
DRINKS: Full Bar
SERVING: Dinner
PRICE RANGE: $$$
NEIGHBORHOOD: Somerville
Modern décor offering a menu of Middle Eastern favorites. Favorites: Brisket Shwarma and Mushroom Mousaka. But oddly enough, if you're there when they are cooking up the fried chicken, get it. Menu of creative cocktails and beers on draft.

SHAMROCK PUB
501 E 8th St, South Boston, 617-268-0007
www.ShamrockPubBoston.com
CUISINE: American (Traditional)/Pub
DRINKS: Full Bar
SERVING: Dinner
PRICE RANGE: $$
NEIGHBORHOOD: South Boston
Neighborhood bar and grill offering typical pub menu. Very much a locals' joint. Favorites: Chicken Parmigiana and Steak Tips. Weekly specials. Live entertainment on Saturday nights. Sports on TV screens.

SHŌJŌ
9A Tyler St, 617-423-7888
www.shojoboston.com
CUISINE: Asian Fusion, Japanese
DRINKS: Full Bar
SERVING: Lunch – Thu - Sat, Dinner – Mon – Sat, Closed on Sundays

PRICE RANGE: $$
NEIGHBORHOOD: Chinatown
Late-night gastropub offering a menu of modern
Asian cuisine with a high energy ambience. Favorites:
Monkey wings and Pork dumplings. Great cocktails
with an impressive selection of Japanese Whiskey.
Reservations recommended.

SILVERTONE
69 Bromfield St, Boston, 617-338-7887
www.silvertonedowntown.com
CUISINE: American (traditional)
DRINKS: Full Bar
SERVING: Dinner nightly except Sun, Lunch Mon -
Fri
PRICE RANGE: $$
NEIGHBORHOOD: Downtown
Comfortable subterranean eatery with a great menu of
comfort food like mac and cheese with chicken. Great
creative cocktails, large portions, and the price is
right.

SPORTELLO
348 Congress St, 617-737-1234
www.sportelloboston.com
CUISINE: Italian
DRINKS: Wine Bar
SERVING: Lunch, & Dinner
PRICE RANGE: $$$
NEIGHBORHOOD: Seaport District
Upscale modern diner with its white-white-white
décor doesn't really obscure a menu of featuring fresh
pastas (hand made here daily) and housemade baked

goods of the absolute highest quality. Favorites: Strozzapreti (braised rabbit with picholine olives & rosemary—I love this dish—it's those excellent olives that make the difference); Potato Gnocchi with lobster & mushroom ragu; Tagliatelle Bolognese. Impressive selection of Italian wines. It's more fun to sit at the counter here and watch the crew work than it is to sit at one of those hours-long marathons where the cooks are like ballet dancers or actors and the price through the roof.

THE TABLE AT SEASON TO TASTE
2447 Massachusetts Ave, 617-871-9468
www.cambridgetable.com
CUISINE: American (New)
DRINKS: Beer & Wine
SERVING: Dinner, Closed Sun & Mon
PRICE RANGE: $$$$
NEIGHBORHOOD: Cambridge
Intimate contemporary eatery offering an ever-changing four course prix fixe menu from one of the area's top chefs. (But you can get small plates at the wine bar if you don't want to sit for the whole shebang—this way you get a feel for the place, which is what I did on my first visit. I came back for more, however.) I suggest booking a table, especially weekends, in this cozy little barebones spot with weathered wooden tables that could use a coat of dark stain, but who cares when the food is this superlative? Favorites: Flank Steak; Lamb shank (so juicy and flavorful); Glazed local halibut, though menu changes quite frequently, based on what's fresh from this

seasonally-oriented spot. Delicious desserts. Extensive wine list.

TANAM
1 Bow Market Way, 617-669-2144
www.tanam.co
CUISINE: Filipino, American (Traditional), Cocktail Bars
DRINKS: Full Bar
SERVING: Dinner, Closed Mon & Tues
PRICE RANGE: $$$
NEIGHBORHOOD: Somerville / Union Square
Food and arts space offering Filipino American cuisine in an eatery actually owned by the workers here, who are obviously among the most hands-on of any place I've been. 5-course fixed-price menu changes often. Favorites: Braised pork shoulder; Blood pudding; Seafood Tinola (soup); Lobster spring roll and Duck confit. They take a lot of pride, justifiably so, in their drinks menu, so take a close look when you visit. Communal seating.

TASTING COUNTER
14 Tyler St, 617-299-6362
www.tastingcounter.com
CUISINE: American (New)
DRINKS: Wine Bar
SERVING: Lunch, & Dinner, Closed Sun & Mon
PRICE RANGE: $$$$
NEIGHBORHOOD: Somerville
Ultra-modern eatery offering a unique pre-paid multi-course dining experience (2 seatings per night). This is one of those places where you sit at the counter

(like it or not) and watch as your meal is prepared—
painstakingly prepared, I should say, with the very
best ingredients. Tickets (you have to pay in advance
online) come with a beverage pairing. Tasting Menu
– 3-course lunch and 9-course dinner available. They
have something called "wine bar hours," which
allows you to slide in here, with no advance notice, to
try a few small plates (smoked duck sandwich, let's
say, or seaweed dumplings) or full-courses (molasses
glazed amberjack), or whatever they happen to have
on offer. (This is a lot of fun.)

TATTE II
318 Third St., Cambridge, 617-354-4200,
www.tattebakery.com
CUISINE: Bakery
DRINKS: No Booze
SERVING: Breakfast & Lunch
PRICE RANGE: $$$
NEIGHBORHOOD: Kendall Square
Friendly bakery that is an ideal choice for breakfast.
Nice assortment of pastries and baked goods. If
you're having breakfast try the breakfast sandwich –
it's the best.

TIGER MAMA
1363 Boylston St, 617-425-6262
www.tigermamaboston.com
CUISINE: Thai, Vietnamese
DRINKS: Full Bar
SERVING: Dinner, Lunch & Dinner on Sundays
PRICE RANGE: $$$
NEIGHBORHOOD: Fenway/Kenmore

Funky eatery with outlandishly fun décor elements offering inspired Southeastern Asian cuisine. Plenty of vegetarian options. Favorites: Pad Gra Pow - Spicy basil with ground chicken and Spicy Eggplant. Classic Tiki cocktails. Drag Brunch on Sundays.

TONY C'S

1265 Boylston St, Boston, 617-236-7369
https://www.tonycssportsbar.com/
CUISINE: Sports Bars/Sandwiches

DRINKS: Full Bar

SERVING: Dinner nightly, Lunch Thurs - Sat
PRICE RANGE: $$$
NEIGHBORHOOD: Fenway
Large sports bar with lots of screens owned by former baseball player Jerry Remy. Features a menu of classic pub grub like crab cakes and BBQ wings. Wide variety of beer on tap. Great view of the ballpark from the rooftop deck.

TORO

1704 Washington St, 617-536-4300
www.toro-restaurant.com
CUISINE: Tapas, Spanish; heavy on Seafood
DRINKS: Full Bar
SERVING: Lunch, & Dinner; Dinner only on Saturdays
PRICE RANGE: $$$
NEIGHBORHOOD: South End
Small eatery (really popular and hard to get into) offering a menu of tapas, seafood, meats and vegetarian dishes. Bar seating as well. Favorites: Small Paella (enough for two) and Costillas de

Cordero (lamb ribs). Cocktails and Spanish wines.
Pitchers of Sangria available (not on menu). Outdoor
seating beneath the blue awning and brick façade in
good weather.

TRESCA
233 Hanover St, Boston, 617-742-8240
www.trescanorthend.com
CUISINE: Italian
DRINKS: Full Bar
SERVING: Dinner nightly, Lunch on Sat
PRICE RANGE: $$$
NEIGHBORHOOD: North End
In the heart of the Italian district, this upscale Tuscan-
inspired eatery offers a creative menu of Italian fare.
The pasta here is all homemade. Menu picks include:
Surf & turf and Pan-fried Lobster. Delicious bread –
be careful, safe room for dessert.

TROQUET

107 South St, Boston, 617-695-9463
www.troquetboston.com
CUISINE: French
DRINKS: Full Bar
SERVING: Dinner
PRICE RANGE: $$$$
NEIGHBORHOOD: Leather District

It is a wine bar serving a variety of half and full
glasses along with bottles of wine paired with its
French menu. The food is as fabulous as its
atmosphere. A highlight I'm partial to is the excellent
roast suckling pig. Quite expensive.

UNION OYSTER HOUSE
41 Union St, Boston, 617-227-2750
www.unionoysterhouse.com
CUISINE: Seafood
DRINKS: Full Bar
SERVING: Lunch, Dinner
PRICE RANGE: $$$
As the oldest restaurant in Boston and the oldest
continuously operating restaurant in the U.S., the
Union Oyster House has been serving diners since
1826. Delicious classic seafood dishes served in
historic setting. Seafood favorites include: Clam
Chowder, Mussels, and Crab Cake, Fish Cake, and
Lobster Cake.

WARREN TAVERN
2 Pleasant St, Charlestown, 617-241-8142
www.warrentavern.com

CUISINE: American (Traditional)
DRINKS: Full Bar
SERVING: Lunch & Dinner
PRICE RANGE: $$
NEIGHBORHOOD: Charlestown
Legendary 1780 tavern still attracts locals and tourists for beer, varied pub food & Colonial charm. Menu of traditional American fare with clever names. Great burgers and Guinness along with a few local craft beers.

WAYPOINT
1030 Massachusetts Ave, 617-864-2300
www.waypointharvard.com
CUISINE: American (New), Seafood
DRINKS: Full Bar
SERVING: Lunch, & Dinner, Dinner only on Saturdays
PRICE RANGE: $$$
NEIGHBORHOOD: Cambridge / Harvard Square
Hip eatery (high dark beamed ceiling, generous bar seating, booths against the wall) offering creative seafood & raw-bar selections in an atmosphere that gives you an authentic sense of the kind of place that filled Harvard Square years ago. Offerings range from simple (pizzas & pastas, Smoked & salted peel & eat shrimp) to more upscale and serious (smoked bluefish, roasted tomato pie that will knock your socks off, if you're wearing socks, and wood-grilled octopus and even, unusually, full caviar service). Larger cuts of roasted meats serve 2 or 3 (think lamb shoulder or whole roasted fish or Creekstone Ribeye). Impressive absinthe menu.

YUME WO KATARE

1923 Massachusetts Ave, Cambridge, 617-714-4008
www.yumewokatare.com
CUISINE: Ramen
DRINKS: No Booze
SERVING: Lunch & Dinner; closed Sun & Mon
PRICE RANGE: $
NEIGHBORHOOD: Porter Square
Popular Japanese eatery with counter service offering
top-notch noodles in huge bowls. The only other
thing on the menu is pork belly available in 2 or 5
pieces. The unique thing about this place is that they
expect you to stand up and announce your dream
when you finish your bowl of noodles.

Chapter 5
NIGHTLIFE

THE BEEHIVE
541 Tremont St, 617-423-0069
www.beehiveboston.com
A restaurant where the lights are low and bands are
chill. Go downstairs to be closer to the band, or stick
to the quieter bar upstairs. Either way, don't leave

without catching the intricate, hand-painted bathroom walls.

DRINK
348 Congress St, Boston, 617-695-1806
www.drinkfortpoint.com
NEIGHBORHOOD: Waterfront, South Boston
Tired of forking over $15 or more for a cocktail that doesn't quite speak to your individual tastes? Then pull up where mixology becomes personal. Instead of providing menus, bartenders ask patrons about their tastes and liquors of choice, and try to concoct the perfect tincture. The bar is reminiscent of a booze-drenched chemistry lab, and any experiments that don't turn out right can be sent back. You can't go wrong with the "Maximilian Affair", a smoky combination of Mezcal, St. Germain, Punt e Mes and lemon juice. When they first opened, they had 3 separate areas, each one emphasizing the cocktails from a different era.

DEEP ELLUM
477 Cambridge St (between Beacon St & Brighton Ave), Allston, 617-787-2337
www.deepellum-boston.com
NEIGHBORHOOD: Allston, Brighton
Beer lovers, on the other hand, should head to Allston, an elegant pub with 28 taps that regularly rotate with Massachusetts breweries like Pretty Things Beer and Ale Project.

GOOD LIFE
28 Kingston St (between Bedford St & Summer St), Boston, 617-451-2622
www.goodlifebar.com
The Good Life is a hidden gem, located in Boston's financial district. They offer an oft-changing menu of

high quality food in their simple/chic dining room. Guests can also enjoy visiting their unique downstairs vodka lounge that features over 150 different types. Various music acts featured nightly downstairs. No Cover Charge.

HALEY HENRY
45 Province St, Boston, 617-208-6000
www.haleyhenry.com
NEIGHBORHOOD: Downtown
Stylish wine bar with a clever menu of snacks that mostly come from canned goods. The chef here has to work cooking on portable burners. The wine list is a bit unusual and they sell sardines by the tin.

JJ FOLEY'S
117 E Berkeley St (between Fay St & Washington St), Boston, 617-728-9101

www.jjfoleyscafe.com
NEIGHBORHOOD: South End
Hard-drinking Irish bar for the downtown crowd.

LUCKY'S LOUNGE
355 Congress St, Boston, 617-357-5825
https://luckyslounge.com/
NEIGHBORHOOD: South Boston/Waterfront
Sinatra-themed lounge with a menu of American comfort food. (Note: there's not a sign out front). Great hangout with classic cocktails and nice beer list.

PARADISE ROCK CLUB
967 Commonwealth Ave, Boston, 617-562-8800
www.paradiserock.club
NEIGHBORHOOD: Allston/Brighton
Next to Boston U., there's this 933-capacity music venue with a rotating roster of top local rock and alternative performers as well as American bands on tour. Get there early if you want a good spot in this basement venue.

WALLY'S CAFÉ JAZZ CLUB
427 Massachusetts Ave, Boston, 617-424-1408
www.wallyscafe.com
NEIGHBORHOOD: South End
Old-school jazz & blues club featuring nightly performances. One of the oldest family owned and operated jazz clubs in existence. (People like Billie Holiday and Charlie Parker played here back in the day.) Schedule includes mostly local acts but check the calendar for national acts. Open every night.

Chapter 6
WHAT TO SEE & DO

BOSTON ATHENAEUM
10 1/2 Beacon St, Boston, 617-227-0270
www.bostonathenaeum.org
NEIGHBORHOOD: Downtown
One of the oldest independent libraries in the United
States. Only a few rooms open to non-members but
it's worth checking out. Notable is the rare book
collection of over 600,000 volumes, an art collection
of 10,000 paintings, sculptures, prints, drawings,
photographs, and decorative arts. Special treasures
include the largest portion of President George
Washington's library from Mount Vernon; Houdon
busts of Washington, Benjamin Franklin, and
Lafayette once owned by Thomas Jefferson; and a
first edition copy of Audubon's "Birds of America."

BOSTON CHOCOLATE TOURS

617-942-0353

www.bostonchocolatetours.com

WEBSITE DOWN AT PRESSTIME

NEIGHBORHOOD: Harvard Square

A variety of tours are offered – all lead by the company's choco-guides – all chocolate lovers. Take a walking tour as you visit a variety of boutique chocolatiers and enjoy Boston's unique cacao-based experiences. If you want more than a tour, they can get you into a Saturday chocolate making workshop. That's really fun.

BOSTON COMMON

Bound by Tremont, Beacon, Charles and Boylston Streets

Boston, No Phone

www.cityofboston.gov/parks/emerald/Boston_Comm
on.asp
Founded in 1634, this is one of the oldest public parks
in the United States. Over the years, many large
gatherings have been held here, from British
encampments in the revolutionary period to anti-war
protests in the 1960s. A nice spot for walking around
and people-watching at all times of year. The Frog
Pond in the center of the Common has wading in the
summer and ice skating in the winter.

BOSTON HARBORWALK
Boston, 617-482-1722
www.bostonharborwalk.com
NEIGHBORHOOD: North End
A public walkway that follows the edge of piers,
wharves, beaches, and shoreline around Boston
Harbor with a spanning distance from Charlestown to
the Dorchester coast. The walkway will be 47 miles
long once completes with 39 miles currently
accessible to visitors.

COMMUNITY BOATING, INC

21 David G Mugar Way, Boston, 617-523-1038
www.community-boating.org
NEIGHBORHOOD: Beacon Hill
The Charles River is cleaning up nicely. Relive your
Head of the Charles days and rent a kayak for $35 a
day. Paddle out for some of the best views of Boston
and Cambridge. Sunny days are spectacular, with
light bouncing off the gold-domed State House and
the city's skyscrapers casting shadows on the intricate
architecture of the Back Bay. The city has never
looked so futuristic.

FANUEIL HALL

www.nps.gov/bost/historyculture/fh.htm
First built in 1742 as an old market building at the
town dock. Town meetings, held here between 1764
and 1774, heard Samuel Adams and others lead cries
of protest against the imposition of taxes on the
colonies. The building was enlarged in 1806.
Frederick Douglass, William Lloyd Garrison, and
Lucy Stone brought their struggles for freedom here

in the 19th century. Market stalls on the first floor service shoppers much as they did in Paul Revere's day. Free.

FENWAY PARK
4 Yawkey Way, Boston, 877-733-7699
https://www.mlb.com/redsox/ballpark
NEIGHBORHOOD: Fenway
All baseball fans know Fenway Park. This is as holy a place in Baseball as Yankee stadium, but at over a century, this is the oldest ballpark in Major League Baseball, and one of the most charming. They've done little to change the place, and that is as it should be. They did add bleachers over the Green Monster in left field, but even with the big video screen, the small park atmosphere remains unchanged. The best way to see this park is to buy tickets to a game. The whole experience is work the price. Even bad seats are good seats here. There are also tours offered, depending on the season. See below.

FENWAY PARK TOURS

4 Yawkey Way, Boston, 866-800-1275
https://www.mlb.com/redsox/ballpark/tours
NEIGHBORHOOD: Fenway
Baseball fans love touring Fenway Park. Going to a game isn't enough when you can go behind the scenes and hear little history about the home of Red Sox Legends, visit Pesky's Pole and sit atop the world famous Green Monster – standing 37 feet 2 inches high overlooking leftfield. Tour guides offer a one hour walking tour of Fenway Park with interesting stories and history. Tours start at the top of each hour. Last tour departs three hours before game time (on game days only).

FREEDOM TRAIL GUIDED TOURS

99 Chauncy St #401, Boston, 617-357-8300
www.thefreedomtrail.org
HOURS: Tours Daily – Check website
ADMISSION: Nominal fee
NEIGHBORHOOD: Harvard Square
This 90-minute tour of the historical 2.5 mile trail that includes Boston's most historic sites is led by guides (wearing Colonial garb) who are very knowledgeable and bring history to life. Admission does not include entry into Freedom Trail sites. Variety of tours available.

GRANARY BURYING GROUND

Tremont St & Bromfield St, Boston, 617-635-7389

NEIGHBORHOOD: Downtown
Many famous figures from the American Revolution are buried here, including Paul Revere, Samuel Adams, John Hancock, and Crispus Attucks.

INSTITUTE OF CONTEMPORARY ART
25 Harbor Shore Dr, Boston, 617-478-3100
www.icaboston.org
NEIGHBORHOOD: Waterfront, South Boston
In a city this historic, it's not every day that a new neighborhood is built from scratch. But that is essentially the story with Fan Pier, a former industrial blight on the South Boston waterfront being transformed, albeit slowly, into a hub of fashion, art and dining. A glass-and-steel museum that seems to hover over the harbor, it is becoming the go-to place for the cool crowd. Check out the gift shop here for

unusual items like cuff links made from the parquet floors of the old Boston Garden.

ISABELLA STEWART GARDNER MUSEUM
25 Evans Way, Boston, 617-566-1401
www.gardnermuseum.org
HOURS: Open daily
ADMISSION: Nominal admission fee, but free to anyone named Isabella, a nice touch
NEIGHBORHOOD: Fenway
This historic museum houses an art collection of world importance including American, Asian, and European art, paintings, sculptures, tapestries, and decorative arts. The museum hosts revolving exhibitions as well as concerts, lectures, and community programs.

KING'S CHAPEL
58 Tremont St (between Somerset St & Beacon St), Boston, 617-523-1749
www.kings-chapel.org
NEIGHBORHOOD: Downtown
Founded as an Anglican congregation in 1686. The bell in the bell tower was originally hung in 1772, cracked in 1814, and was recast by Paul Revere in 1816: this bell is still in use today. King's Chapel Burying Ground: Predating King's Chapel, this cemetery was founded in 1630, and is the oldest in Boston. Notable figures buried here include John Winthrop and William Dawes.

MASSACHUSETTS STATE HOUSE
24 Beacon St, Boston, 617-722-2000
www.sec.state.ma.us/trs/trsbok/trstour.htm
NEIGHBORHOOD: Beacon Hill
Monday - Friday: 10:00 - 16:00. The Massachusetts
State House was built in 1781 on top of land once
owned by John Hancock. The dome of the State
House was recently refurbished with glittering gold
leaf, and makes for a spectacular view at sunset from
the Massachusetts Avenue Bridge.

MUSEUM OF FINE ARTS
465 Huntington Ave, Boston, 617-267-9300
www.mfa.org
NEIGHBORHOOD: Huntington Ave
Boston's oldest, largest and best-known art institution,
this museum boasts one of the world's most
comprehensive art collections – nearly 450,000 works

of art, from furniture to jewelry to coins. The museum, known for its Impressionist paintings, Asian and Egyptian collections, and early American art, first opened its doors on July 4, 1876. Kids tend to love the collection of mummies.

MUSEUM OF SCIENCE
1 Science Park, Boston, 617-723-2500
www.mos.org
NEIGHBORHOOD: Harvard Square
Located in Science Park, this Boston landmark features over 700 interactive exhibitions. The museum also offers several live presentations daily along with shows at the **Charles Hayden Planetarium** and the **Mugar Omni Theater**. Other features of the museum include: the Butterfly Garden, the collection of optical illusions, and many other fascinating exhibitions unique to this museum, some of them interactive.

NICHOLS HOUSE MUSEUM
55 Mount Vernon St, 617-227-6993
www.nicholshousemuseum.org
NEIGHBORHOOD: Beacon Hill
HOURS: Open 11 a.m. – 4 p.m. daily
ADMISSION: Minimal admission fee
This museum is the 1804 townhouse that was once the home of Rose Standish Nichols – a landscape gardener, suffragist and pacifist. The four-story town house features a collection of fine European and American wooden furniture from the 17th -19th centuries, ancestral portraits, Flemish tapestries, oriental rugs, European and Asian art, and works by

sculptor Augustus Saint-Gaudens. The museum offers a schedule of lectures, programs, and special events. Guided tours are available.

OLD SOUTH MEETING HOUSE
310 Washington St, Boston, 617-482-6439
www.osmh.org
NEIGHBORHOOD: Downtown
9:30 AM to 5 PM (Apr-Oct), 10 AM to 4 PM (Nov-Mar). An important meeting place for centuries: currently a museum. In 1773, a group of colonists attacked a tea ship after a meeting here, in what became known as the Boston Tea Party. $5.

OLD STATE HOUSE
206 Washington St (between Court St & State St),
Boston, 617-720-1713
www.bostonhistory.org
NEIGHBORHOOD: Downtown
9 AM to 5 PM (4 PM in Jan, 6 PM in July and
Aug). The former seat of government in Boston, and
the oldest surviving building. In 1770, the Boston
Massacre took place just in front of the State House,

and in 1776 the Declaration of Independence was first
read to Bostonians from the balcony.

PARK STREET CHURCH
1 Park St (between Park St Place &Tremont St),
Boston, 617-523-3383
www.parkstreet.org
NEIGHBORHOOD: Downtown
Founded in 1809, and still an active house of worship,
this church is known for a number of historical firsts.
Among other things, William Lloyd Garrison
delivered his first anti-slavery address here, and "My
Country Tis of Thee" was first sung on the front
steps.

ROSE FITZGERALD KENNEDY GREENWAY
Atlantic Ave, Boston, 617-292-0020
www.rosekennedygreenway.org

Downtown was once defined by an elevated steel highway. Then by the Big Dig, the seemingly never-ending project to sink the roadway underground. After billions of dollars and an untold numbers of delays, it is finally home to the mile-long ribbon of lawns, public art and much-needed playgrounds snaking along Atlantic Avenue. To explore this emerald oasis, start at South Station and meander toward the North End, stopping to frolic in the fountains or take a spin on the carousel. At Christopher Columbus Park, find a spot under a wisteria-covered trellis and watch as boats bob in the harbor and planes take off from Logan Airport. It's been worth the wait.

SWAN BOATS
4 Charles St, Boston, 617-522-1966
Public Garden Lagoon
www.swanboats.com
HOURS: Open every day, weather permitting.

ADMISSION: Small admission fee
NEIGHBORHOOD: Harvard Square
Boston's iconic Swan Boat ride lasts only about 15 minutes but is a must for any visitor, though I have to admit I've never done it.

Chapter 7
SHOPPING & SERVICES

BOBBY FROM BOSTON
545 Washington St, Lynn, 617-423-9299
www.bobbyfrombostonvintage.com
NEIGHBORHOOD: South End
Great for men's high-end vintage fashions like ties
and jackets. Small selection of women's clothing.

BODEGA
6 Clearway St, Boston, 617-421-1550
www.bdgastore.com
NEIGHBORHOOD: Hynes Convention Center
Station
Hidden behind an entrance disguised as a
convenience store (with cereal boxes in the window),

this curated boutique offers hipsters a variety of fashions, shoes, caps and sportswear. You have to open up the Snapple vending machine door to get into the store. Labels include: Headporter plus, Nike, Adidas, vans, Yuketen, Stussy, Mishka, and Original Fake.

COPLEY PLACE
110 Huntington Av, Boston, 617-262-6600
http://www.simon.com/mall/copley-place
NEIGHBORHOOD: Back Bay
Here you will find a huge Shopping Center including your famous brands such as Dior, Hugo Boss, Jimmy Choo, Louis Vuitton, Sony, Barneys, Tiffany, Armani among others.

FANEUIL HALL MARKETPLACE
4 S Market Building, Boston, 617-523-1300
www.faneuilhallmarketplace.com
NEIGHBORHOOD: Financial District
Come and explore for yourself. Lots of shops and vendors. Super touristy spot.

FLOCK
274 Shawmut Ave, Boston, 617-391-0222
www.flockboston.com
NEIGHBORHOOD: South End
A beautiful eclectic shop for women run by a mother-daughter team. Here you'll find flowing dresses, rocker tees, baby doll dresses, and lots of whimsical gifts and accessories.

G-STAR RAW STORE
160 Newbury St (between Dartmouth St & Exeter St), Boston, 617-867-6505
www.g-star.com
NEIGHBORHOOD: Back Bay
For men and women.

GARY DRUG CO
59 Charles St, Boston, 617-227-0023
www.garydrug.com
NEIGHBORHOOD: Beacon Hill
Since the 1930s, this family-run pharmacy has offered
medical and beauty supplies, wheelchairs, and home
care supplies. It's one of the last remaining family-
run pharmacies in the country. Worth visiting just to
feel like you're going back in time, look for the
forest-green wooden sign out front.

IN-JEAN-IUS
441 Hanover St, Boston, 617-523-5326
www.injeanius.com
NEIGHBORHOOD: North End
Where the friendly staff stops at nothing to turn up
that perfect pair.

SAULT NEW ENGLAND
577 Tremont St, Boston, 857-239-9434
www.saultne.com
NEIGHBORHOOD: South End
A unique men's shop featuring fashions, gifts, and a selection of curated vintage items. This place has the feel of a General Store with unusual items such as beard balms, pocket combs, and wooden iPhone accessories.

SOWA OPEN MARKET
530 Harrison Ave, Boston, 857-362-7692
www.sowaboston.com

NEIGHBORHOOD: Harvard Square
Outdoor flea market featuring a eclectic selection of
crafts vendors on Sundays May through October.
Here you'll find fashions, furnishings, jewelry, art,
food from a variety of artisans and much more.

INDEX

T

U

W

Y

How About Some Free Thrillers?

Besides his travel & restautant guides, the author also writes page-turning political thrillers.

Send him an email and he'll send you the **first 3** in his bestselling series **FREE**.

Why, you ask, would he do something so foolish?

Because he's sure he'll get you hooked.

andrewdelaplaine@mac.com

CPSIA information can be obtained
at www.ICGtesting.com
Printed in the USA
LVHW010732300721
694026LV00011B/969